HANDS-ON JOBS

SANITATION WORKERS

ANNE FOREST

PowerKiDS press
New York

Published in 2016 by The Rosen Publishing Group, Inc.
29 East 21st Street, New York, NY 10010

First Edition

Editor: Katie Kawa
Book Design: Reann Nye

Photo Credits: Cover, pp. 3–24 (background texture) Toluk/Shutterstock.com; cover, pp. 13 (top), 17 Don Mason/Blend Images/Getty Images; pp. 5, 7 (bottom) Dmitry Kalinovsky/Shutterstock.com; p. 7 (top) FashionStock.com/Shutterstock.com; p. 9 (top) JACQUES DEMARTHON/AFP/Getty Images; p. 9 (bottom) © iStockphoto.com/SunChan; p. 11 Pangfolio.com/Shutterstock.com; p. 13 (bottom) Paul Vasarhelyi/Shutterstock.com; p. 15 Caz Harris Photography/Shutterstock.com; p. 19 Konstanttin/Shutterstock.com; p. 21 © iStockphoto.com/Alex Potemkin; p. 22 wavebreakmedia/Shutterstock.com.

Cataloging-in-Publication Data

Forest, Anne.
Sanitation workers / by Anne Forest.
p. cm. — (Hands-on jobs)
Includes index.
ISBN 978-1-5081-4371-0 (pbk.)
ISBN 978-1-5081-4372-7 (6-pack)
ISBN 978-1-5081-4373-4 (library binding)
1. Sanitation workers — Juvenile literature. 2. Refuse and refuse disposal — Juvenile literature. I. Title.
HD8039.S257 F67 2016
628.4'42'023—d23

Manufactured in the United States of America

CPSIA Compliance Information: Batch #BW16PK: For Further Information contact Rosen Publishing, New York, New York at 1-800-237-9932

CONTENTS

KEEPING COMMUNITIES CLEAN

Keeping cities and towns clean isn't an easy job, but it's a necessary one. Sanitation workers **perform** different tasks in their community to keep it clean. Some sanitation workers are garbage collectors, while others collect recyclable **materials**. Sanitation workers in some communities do many jobs, including collecting garbage and recyclable materials, removing snow, and cleaning streets.

Sanitation workers are important parts of every community. If you're willing to get your hands dirty to keep your city or town clean, this might be a good career for you. Read on to learn more about what it takes to be a sanitation worker!

DIGGING DEEPER

Americans throw out over 250 million tons (226,796,185 mt) of trash each year. Just think where we would be without sanitation workers!

Garbage collection is a dirty job, but sanitation workers make a good living for their hard work.

MAKING A DIFFERENCE

Sanitation workers do more than just make their community look nicer by picking up trash. They help people in their community stay safe and healthy, too. In places where it snows, sanitation workers often **plow** the streets to remove snow. They also spread salt and sand on icy roads to keep cars from sliding. This helps people in cars stay safe when driving conditions are **dangerous**.

By cleaning up garbage, sanitation workers keep diseases, or sicknesses, from spreading. Disease-causing bacteria can grow in garbage. Bugs and other animals that spread disease can make their home in uncollected trash, too.

DIGGING DEEPER

Flies, raccoons, and rats are often found around trash that hasn't been collected. They're known to carry and spread diseases.

Sanitation workers play an important part in matters of public safety and health. Without sanitation workers, there would be more car crashes in the winter and more diseases spread around cities and towns.

THE WAY THEY WORK

If you're interested in a career as a sanitation worker, who would you be working for? Sanitation workers generally work for private sanitation companies or local governments. Sometimes, the companies and governments work together to keep places clean.

Sanitation workers generally follow set **routes** and pick up garbage or recyclable materials from certain neighborhoods on certain days. The people who live in these neighborhoods know what day to take their trash to the curb to be picked up by sanitation workers. Sometimes, sanitation workers who work for a private company will collect trash or recyclable materials after someone makes an appointment.

DIGGING DEEPER

Sanitation workers often start working very early in the morning. They often start collecting garbage or cleaning streets before the sun rises! If a winter storm is bad, workers who plow streets might need to work overnight.

Sanitation workers can be found in all communities—from the largest cities to the smallest neighborhoods.

GETTING RID OF GARBAGE

Garbage collectors are a familiar kind of sanitation worker. They can be seen hard at work in neighborhoods all over the world. In small communities, garbage collectors sometimes work alone. They drive the garbage truck and load the garbage into it themselves. However, in many communities, teams of sanitation workers are needed to take trash away.

One worker drives the garbage truck, and they must have a special **license** to do so. Other workers pick up garbage bags or cans from the curb and empty them into the truck. These workers must be strong enough to lift heavy bags and cans of garbage.

DIGGING DEEPER

People sometimes throw hazardous, or dangerous, materials away with the rest of their trash. These include certain cleaners, batteries, and paint. Sanitation workers must be trained to safely handle and get rid of these materials.

Sanitation workers learn most of the skills they need on the job. They learn to take garbage from people's homes and businesses to a landfill, which is a place where waste is buried. They can also take garbage to an incinerator, which is a machine that burns waste, such as the one shown here.

INSIDE A GARBAGE TRUCK

Sanitation workers are often seen riding on the back or side of a garbage truck. Garbage trucks play a big part in helping sanitation workers do their job. Not every sanitation worker is licensed to drive one of these trucks, but any sanitation worker who collects garbage needs to know how they work.

A garbage truck has a part called a hopper, which is where sanitation workers dump the garbage. Some hoppers have a special blade for pressing down on the garbage to make room for more trash. These hoppers are called compactors.

DIGGING DEEPER

Some garbage trucks use mechanical systems to lift and empty garbage cans on their own. Others require a sanitation worker to lift and empty the garbage into the hopper.

Garbage trucks are making use of advanced **technology** to help sanitation workers do their job. Some garbage trucks have electronic **navigation** tools to help sanitation workers plan their route for the day.

READY TO RECYCLE

Recycling is an important part of caring for our planet. Communities often employ sanitation workers whose job is to collect recyclable materials from people's homes and businesses. Common materials collected by these workers include metal, glass, paper, and plastic.

Recyclable material collectors are sanitation workers who pick up these materials just like garbage collectors pick up trash from neighborhoods. Then, they take recyclable items to a materials recovery facility (MRF). At the MRF, the recyclable materials are sorted and then prepared to be made into new products.

DIGGING DEEPER

If recycling is a cause you feel strongly about, you might also be interested in a career as a sorter at an MRF. Sorters separate different types of recyclable materials. However, new sorting technology is taking the place of human sorters at some MRFs.

Sanitation workers also collect recyclable materials from public places, such as parks. The work they do to collect and transport recyclable materials helps the environment.

SANITATION SAFETY

Safety is an area of concern for sanitation workers. Their job can be very dangerous because they work with heavy objects, hazardous materials, and moving **vehicles**.

Sanitation workers have been hurt and even killed by other cars on the road. This is one of the reasons they wear bright vests or other clothing: to be more easily seen. Sanitation workers are also at risk of falling from their own truck when they stand on the side or back of it as it's moving. They should only do this for short periods of time when the truck is traveling at low speeds.

DIGGING DEEPER

Sanitation workers are sometimes hit by their own truck when it's backing up. To avoid this, some trucks have sensors that alert the driver when another sanitation worker is walking behind the truck.

Sanitation workers should wear shoes that keep them from slipping while standing on a moving garbage truck. The truck should also have handles for them to hold while riding.

MORE THAN ONE JOB

Sanitation workers have to be ready to do much more than just collect garbage. In addition to removing snow and treating slippery roads, these workers also operate street-cleaning machines. They need to be familiar with all the **equipment** and vehicles needed to do these jobs, so a basic understanding of mechanics is helpful for sanitation workers.

If you want to work in the field of sanitation and you love science and math, then you might consider a career as a sanitation engineer. A sanitation engineer is also known as a sanitary engineer. This kind of engineer uses their skills at building machines to improve sanitation methods.

DIGGING DEEPER

Sanitation engineers are often environmental engineers. These engineers work to reduce pollution and get rid of hazardous waste in ways that are safer for people and the environment.

WHAT DOES A SANITATION WORKER DO?

- collects garbage
- removes snow
- collects recyclable materials
- operates street-cleaning machines
- spreads salt and sand on slippery roads
- drives vehicles such as garbage trucks and snowplows
- checks trash for hazardous waste and then safely gets rid of it
- keeps records of garbage collections and recyclable material collections

These are some of the many tasks performed by sanitation workers around the United States. Each community's sanitation workers have different jobs, based on the weather and size of the community.

HOW CAN YOU PREPARE?

You can start preparing now for a career as a sanitation worker if this job sounds fun to you. Basic reading and math skills are important for this job, so continue to pay attention in school. Environmental science also plays a big part in this line of work. Learning as much as you can about this branch of science is helpful if you want to become a sanitation worker.

If you ever get a chance to see sanitation workers on the job, pay attention to what they're doing. Sanitation workers learn their job by watching others, and you can learn about this career by watching them, too.

DIGGING DEEPER

Sanitation workers need to be strong to do their job well. Exercising now will help you stay fit to follow this career path in the future.

People interested in a career as a sanitation worker should like working outdoors. Sanitation workers spend most of their workday outside. They work in all kinds of weather—from high heat and rain to cold winds and snow.

A MESS WITHOUT THEM

Another way to prepare for this career path is to recycle. Learning about recycling and the types of materials that can be recycled won't just help you with your future career—it will help the environment, too! By recycling, you'll be working to keep your community clean for a long time, which is also what sanitation workers do.

Sanitation workers have a career that can be dirty and dangerous. However, they know the work they're doing for their communities is worth the risk. Our cities and towns would be a mess without the efforts of sanitation workers!

GLOSSARY

dangerous: Not safe.

environment: The natural world around us.

equipment: The tools needed for a certain purpose.

license: An official paper giving someone the right to do something.

material: Something from which something else can be made.

navigation: The act or process of finding the way to get to a place when you are traveling.

perform: To do an activity that often requires training or skill.

plow: To use a snowplow to remove snow from a road.

route: A road or course of travel from one place to another.

technology: The use of science to solve problems.

vehicle: A machine used to carry goods from one place to another.

INDEX

WEBSITES

Due to the changing nature of Internet links, PowerKids Press has developed an online list of websites related to the subject of this book. This site is updated regularly. Please use this link to access the list: www.powerkidslinks.com/hoj/sanwk